ex libris

....

PENGUIN BOOKS

Published by the Penguin Group
Penguin Books Ltd
27 Wrights Lane, London W8 5TZ, England
Penguin Books USA Inc.
375 Hudson Street, New York, New York 10014, USA
Penguin Books Australia Ltd
Ringwood, Victoria, Australia
Penguin Books Canada Ltd
10 Alcorn Avenue, Toronto, Ontario, Canada M4V 3B2
Penguin Books (NZ) Ltd
182–190 Wairau Road, Auckland 10, New Zealand
Penguin Books Ltd
Registered Offices: Harmondsworth, Middlesex, England

First published by Penguin Books Australia Ltd 1997
3 5 7 9 10 8 6 4

This selection copyright © Penguin Books Australia Ltd 1997

Printed in England by William Clowes Ltd

the little book of
LOVE

When love beckons you, follow him,
Though his ways are hard and steep.
And when his wings enfold you,
yield to him,
Though the sword hidden among
his pinions may wound you.
And when he speaks to you,
believe him,
Though his voice may shatter
your dreams as the north wind
lays waste in the garden.

Kahlil Gibran

Love is all we have, the only way
that each can help the other.

Euripides

Love those who love you.

Voltaire

Love is a pleasing but
a various clime.

William Shenstone

You are always new.
The last of your kisses
was ever the sweetest . . .

John Keats

If the heart of a man is
depressed with cares,
The mist is dispelled when
a woman appears.

John Gay

All thoughts, all passions,
all delights,
Whatever stirs this mortal frame,
All are but ministers of Love,
And feed his sacred flame.

Samuel Taylor Coleridge

All love is sweet,
Given or returned.
Common as light is love,
And its familiar voice wearies
not ever.

Percy Byshhe Shelley

An old man in love is like
a flower in winter.

Chinese proverb

In her first passion woman
loves her lover,
In all the others all she loves
is love.

George Gordon, Lord Byron

And all for love,
and nothing for reward.

Edmund Spenser

Two human loves make
one divine.

Elizabeth Barrett Browning

What of soul was left,
I wonder, when the kissing
had to stop?

Robert Browning

Is it, in heav'n, a crime
to love too well?

Alexander Pope

God is Love – I dare say.
But what a mischievous
devil Love is!

Samuel Butler

For aught that ever I could read,
Could ever hear by tale or history,
The course of true love never did
run smooth.

William Shakespeare

Loving a woman who scorns you is
like licking honey from a thorn.

Welsh proverb

Lord! I wonder what fool it was
that first invented kissing.

Jonathan Swift

She is not fair to outward view
As many maidens be;
Her loveliness I never knew
Until she smiled on me.

Hartley Coleridge

All, everything that I understand,
I understand only because I love.

Leo Tolstoy

Oh, they loved dearly;
their souls kissed,
they kissed with their eyes,
they were both but
one single kiss.

Heinrich Heine

Western Wind, when wilt thou blow,
The small rain down can rain?
Christ if my love were in my arms
And I in my bed again!

Anonymous, 16th Century

Ah! when will this long
weary day have end,
And lend me leave to come
unto my love?

Edmund Spenser

But to see her was to love her,
Love but her, and love for ever.

Robert Burns

A man in love mistakes a harelip for a dimple.

Japanese proverb

Love is blind, and lovers cannot see
The pretty follies that
themselves commit.

William Shakespeare

My flocks feed not,
My ewes breed not,
My rams speed not,
   All is amiss.
Love is dying,
Faith's defying,
Heart's denying,
   Causer of this.

Richard Barnfield

Love is enough:
though the world be awaning,
And the woods have no voice
but the voice of complaining.

William Morris

Love is like the measles;
we all have to go through it.

Jerome K. Jerome

Whoso loves believes
the impossible.

Elizabeth Barrett Browning

Love looks not with the eyes,
but with the mind . . .

William Shakespeare

Ah Love! Could thou and I
with fate conspire
To grasp this sorry Scheme
of Things entire,
Would not we shatter it to bits -
and then
Remould it nearer to the
Heart's Desire!

Edward Fitzgerald

So, we'll go no more a roving
So late into the night,
Though the heart be still as loving,
And the moon be still as bright.

For the sword outweighs its sheath,
And the soul wears out the breast,
And the heart must pause
to breathe,
And love itself have rest.

George Gordon, Lord Byron

Love is swift of foot;
Love's a man of war,
And can shoot,
And can hit from far.

George Herbert

Love is the wisdom of the fool
and the folly of the wise.

Samuel Johnson

A new commandment
I give unto you,
That ye love one another.

St John 13:34

He who binds to himself a joy
Does the winged life destroy
But he who kisses the joy as it flies
Lives in eternity's sun rise.

William Blake

Were the whole realm of
nature mine,
That were a present far too small;
Love so amazing, so divine
Demands my soul, my life, my all.

Isaac Watts

Love sought is good,
but giv'n unsought is better.

William Shakespeare

Lips only sing when they
cannot kiss.

James Thomson

Love is the life of every man.

Emanuel Swedenborg

Love rules the court,
the camp, the grove,
And men below, and saints above;
For love is heaven
and heaven is love.

Sir Walter Scott

Love lives in cottages
as well as in court.

English proverb

Love then, and even later, was the whole concern of everyone's life. That is always the fate of leisured societies.

Napoleon Bonaparte

Friendship is love
without his wings!

George Gordon, Lord Byron

Many waters cannot quench love,
neither can the floods drown it.

Song of Solomon

Give me a thousand kisses, then a hundred, then a thousand more.

Catullus

No, there's nothing half so
sweet in life
As love's young dream.

Thomas Moore

Drinking when we are not thirsty
and making love at all seasons,
madam: that is all there is
to distinguish us from
the other animals.

Pierre-Augustin de Beaumarchais

Love's but the frailty of the mind,
– When 'tis not with
ambition joined.

William Congreve

There is no love like
the first love.

Italian proverb

O, my Luve's like a red red rose
That's newly sprung in June:
O, my Luve's like the melodie
That's sweetly play'd in tune.

Robert Burns

You cannot give a kiss without
taking and cannot take
without giving.

Anonymous

There is no fear in love;
but perfect love casteth out fear.

John, 4:18

You say, to me-wards your
affection's strong;
Pray love me little, so you
love me long.

Robert Herrick

There can be no peace of mind in love, since the advantage one has secured is never anything but a fresh starting-point for further desires.

Marcel Proust

For news of the heart ask the face.

Cambodian proverb

Tomorrow may he love
who never loved before,
and may he who has loved
love too.

Pervigilium Veneris

Doubt thou the stars are fire;
Doubt that the sun doth move;
Doubt truth to be a liar;
But never doubt I love.

William Shakespeare

If music be the food of love, play on;
Give me excess of it, that, surfeiting,
The appetite may sicken, and so die.
That strain again! It had
a dying fall:
O! it came o'er my ear like
the sweet sound
That breathes upon a bank
of violets,
Stealing and giving odour!

William Shakespeare

He spake of love, such love
as spirits feel
In worlds whose course is
equable and pure;
No fears to beat away –
no strife to heal, –
The past unsighed for,
and the future sure.

William Wordsworth

Let him kiss me with the kisses
of his mouth: for thy love
is better than wine.

Song of Solomon, 1:2

Only our love hath no decay;
This, no tomorrow hath,
nor yesterday,
Running it never runs
from us away,
But truly keeps his first, last,
everlasting day.

John Donne

The Summer hath his joys,
And Winter his delights.
Though Love and all his pleasures
are but toys,
They shorten tedious nights.

Thomas Campion

Love seeketh not itself to please,
Nor for itself hath any care,
But for another gives its ease,
And builds a Heaven in
Hell's despair.

William Blake

Love and a cough cannot be hid.

George Herbert

A life without love
is like a year without summer.

Swedish proverb

If thou must love me,
let it be for naught
Except for love's sake only.

Robert Browning

Spice a dish with love and
it pleases every palate.

Plautus

When Love speaks, the voice
of all the gods
Makes heaven drowsy with
the harmony.

William Shakespeare

Tell me whom you love,
and I'll tell you who you are.

African-American proverb

True love's the gift which
God has given
To man alone beneath the heaven.

Sir Walter Scott

We love being in love,
that's the truth on't.

W. M. Thackeray

Freely we serve
Because we freely love, as in
our will
To love or not; in this we
stand or fall.

John Milton

Love consists in desiring to give
what is our own to another and
feeling his delight as our own.

Emanuel Swedenborg

I hold it true, whate'er befall;
I feel it when I sorrow most;
'Tis better to have loved and lost
Than never to have loved at all.

Alfred, Lord Tennyson

She who has never loved
has never lived.

John Gay

Is it so small a thing
To have enjoyed the sun,
To have lived light in the spring,
To have loved, to have thought, to
have done?

Matthew Arnold

Kisses are like grains of gold
or silver found upon the ground,
of no value themselves, but precious
as showing that a mine is near.

Georges Villiers

There is no greater nor keener
pleasure than that of bodily love –
and none which is more rational.

Plato

Love can vanquish Death.

Alfred, Lord Tennyson

If I were pressed to say
why I loved him,
I feel that my only reply could be:
'Because it was he,
because it was I'.

Michel de Montaigne

The supreme happiness of life
is the conviction that we are loved.

Victor Hugo

Who ever loved,
that loved not at first sight?

Christopher Marlowe

Married couples who love each other
tell each other a thousand things
without talking.

Portuguese proverb

He who finds not love
finds nothing.

Chilean proverb

A lover's eyes will gaze
an eagle blind;
A lover's ear will hear
the lowest sound.

William Shakespeare

Alas! the love of women! it is known
To be a lovely and a fearful thing.

George Gordon, Lord Byron

All mankind love a lover.

Ralph Waldo Emerson

More like a man
Flying from something he dreads
than one
Who sought the thing he loved.

William Wordsworth

A thing of beauty is a joy for ever:
Its loveliness increases; it will never
Pass into nothingness.

John Keats

Love is a kind of warfare.

Ovid

Is not old wine wholesomest, old
pippins toothsomest, old wood burn
brightest, old linen wash whitest?
Old soldiers, sweethearts, are surest,
and old lovers are soundest.

John Webster

O lyric Love, half angel
and half bird
And all a wonder and
a wild desire.

Robert Browning

Fill ev'ry glass, for wine
inspires us,
And fires us
With courage, love and joy.
Women and wine should
life employ.
Is there aught else on earth
desirous?

John Gay

Love is a symbol of eternity.
It wipes out all sense of time,
destroying all memory of a
beginning and all fear
of an end.

Madame de Staël

My heart is like a singing bird
Whose nest is in a watered shoot;
My heart is like an apple-tree
Whose boughs are bent with
thickest fruit;
My heart is like a rainbow shell
That paddles in a halcyon sea;
My heart is gladder than all these
Because my love is come to me.

Christina Rosetti

He who desires but acts not
breeds pestilence.

William Blake

Love that is old never rusts.

German proverb

Let me not to the marriage
of true minds
Admit impediments.
Love is not love
Which alters when it
alteration finds,
Or tends with the remover
to remove:
O, no! it is an ever-fixèd mark.

William Shakespeare

Perfect love sometimes does not come until the first grandchild.

Welsh proverb

See the mountains kiss high Heaven
And the waves clasp one another;
No sister-flower would be forgiven
If it disdained its brother;
And the sunlight clasps the earth
And the moonbeams kiss the sea:
What is all this sweet work worth
If thou kiss not me?

Percy Bysshe Shelley

At the touch of love,
everyone becomes a poet.

Plato

Wine comes in at the mouth
And love comes in at the eye;
That's all we know for truth
Before we grow old and die.
I lift the glass to my mouth,
I look at you, and I sigh.

William Butler Yeats

Drink to me only with thine eyes,
And I will pledge with mine;
Or leave a kiss but in the cup
And I'll not look for wine.

Ben Jonson

Those who restrain Desire, do so
because theirs is weak enough
to be restrained.

William Blake

Love, and do what you like.

St Augustine

A loving heart is always young.

French proverb

Who can give law to lovers?
Love is a greater law to itself.

Boethius

Love gives naught but itself and
takes naught but from itself.
Love possesses not nor would
it be possessed;
For love is sufficient unto love.

Kahlil Gibran

The best portion of a good
man's life,
His little, nameless,
unremembered acts
Of kindness and of love.

William Wordsworth

I feel again a spark of that
ancient flame.

Virgil

It is best to cultivate a heart of love
that knows no anger.

Irish proverb

Like the fire of life,
love either consumes
or purifies.

Anonymous

The magic of first love is our
ignorance that it can never end.

Benjamin Disraeli

Live and let love.

Anonymous

Love makes all hard hearts gentle.

George Herbert

Power cannot command love
nor money buy it.

Anonymous

Sex is the poor man's opera.

Italian proverb

The stellar universe is not so
difficult to understand as the real
actions of other people, especially
of the people with whom
we are in love.

Marcel Proust

Familiar acts are beautiful
through love.

Percy Bysshe Shelley

What is it men in women
do require?
The lineaments of Gratified Desire.
What is it women in men
do require?
The lineaments of Gratified Desire.

William Blake

Love is a power too strong to be overcome by anything but flight.

Cervantes

Excellent wretch! Perdition
catch my soul
But I do love thee! And when
I love thee not,
Chaos is come again.

William Shakespeare

How do I love thee? Let me
count the ways.
I love thee to the depth
and breadth of height
My soul can reach, when
feeling out of sight
For the ends of Being and
ideal Grace.

Robert Browning

As for the lover, his soul dwells
in the body of another.

Marcus Cato

Youth's the season made for joys,
Love is then our duty.

John Gay

The day breaks not,
it is my heart.

John Donne

If thou remember'st not
the slightest folly
That ever love did make
thee run into,
Thou has not loved.

William Shakespeare

The intellect is always fooled
by the heart.

Duc de la Rouchefoucauld

Never seek to tell thy love,
Love that never told can be;
For the gentle wind does move
Silently, invisibly.

William Blake

Kisses are like almonds.

Sicilian proverb

Love draws me one way,
reason another.

Ovid

Love is that orbit of the restless soul
Whose circle grazes the
confines of space,
Bounding within the limits
of its race
Utmost extremes.

George Henry Boker

I love thee with a love I
seemed to lose
With my lost saints – I love thee
with the breath,
Smiles, tears, of all my life! –
and if God choose,
I shall but love thee better
after death.

Robert Browning

Oh lift me from the grass!
I die! I faint! I fail!
Let thy love and kisses rain
On my lips and eyelids pale.
My cheek is cold and white, alas!
My heart beats loud and fast; –
Oh! Press it to thine own again,
Where it will break at last.

Percy Bysshe Shelley

Love is a fiend, a fire,
a heaven, a hell,
Where pleasure, pain, and sad
repentance dwell.

Richard Barnfield

If it were not for hopes,
the heart would break.

Thomas Fuller

If you want to be loved,
love and be lovable.

Benjamin Franklin

Love is the blossom
where there blows
Everything that lives or grows.

Giles Fletcher

Love keeps out the cold better
than a cloak. It serves for
food and raiment.

Longfellow

Love in its essence is
spiritual fire.

Emanuel Swedenborg

Love is the god who gives
safety to the city.

Zeno

Love is nothing else but an insatiate thirst of enjoying a greedily desired object.

Montaigne

For loveliness
Needs not the foreign
aid of ornament,
But is, when unadorned,
adorned the most.

James Thomson

True Love is but a humble,
low-born thing,
And hath its food served up in
earthen ware;

It is a thing to walk with,
hand in hand,
Through the everydayness of
this workday world.

J. R. Lowell

Love is the mind's strong physic,
and the pill
That leaves the heart sick and
o'erturns the will.

Thomas Middleton

I love thee like pudding;
if thou wert pie I'd eat thee.

John Ray

The universe hangs on a kiss,
exists in the hold of a kiss.

Zalman Shneor

Rose-leaves, when the rose is dead,
Are heaped for the beloved's bed;
And so thy thoughts, when
thou art gone,
Love itself shall slumber on.

Percy Bysshe Shelley

Tell her, brief is life
but love is long.

Alfred, Lord Tennyson

We were two and had
but one heart.

François Villon

Never love unless you can
Bear with all the faults of man!

Thomas Campion

Let those love now,
who never lov'd before;
Let those who always lov'd,
now love the more.

Thomas Parnell

Keep love in your heart.
A life without it
is like a sunless garden
when the flowers are dead.
The consciousness of loving
and being loved brings
a warmth and richness to life
that nothing else can bring.

Oscar Wilde

A ruddy drop of manly blood
The surging sea outweighs;
The world uncertain comes
and goes,
The lover rooted stays.

Ralph Waldo Emerson